*for Cathy,
always an
inspiration*

Contents

Prelude

*'Law? I've got me
own law, mate.'*

The Immediate

on a needless death, 2018

As the young man ebbed away,
surrounded by those who were his own,
did he see that love was absent,
too late, distracted by the sensual dancers,
the night-club, dark street crooners
praising the affections of a fading moment.
Did he know that they would walk by him?
Was he clocked and fussed and turned away?
How many words of appeal came from him,
or dissolved, as limbs, cries, eyes,
took the place of bland domestic appeals?

Love had worn a mask, dressed in motley.
Love was the drunken singer, begging,
standing by the copper-filled cap.
Love was tired of weeping, sore and weak.
Love had packed her bags and left home.
Love should have been found
in the immediate, dredged from the ocean
of *don't care* and *don't talk to me*.

When we all stand with Whitman,
the immediate will roll out the bloody bandages,
give us the stink of dying,
give us the engulfing tide of caring.
Love will be fished out of the water,
an exhausted whale, thrashing for life,
and it will be tended, mended,
told that it matters again.

When they look back at our failures,
in the time when double-speak has no comfort,
and the official line is incorrect,
will love have been removed,
dropped from the dictionary,
replaced by acronyms hiding truth
like thorns around a berry?
Then we'll feel an emptiness
and that, too, will have no word.

The Overcoat

It was rust, not like the white flesh,
Like he rusted inside.
And it was thick,
Too warm to take off and shiver.
Its mothballs seeped acid into his days.
Without some big coat
He was naked, but deeper than skin.
My uncle.

So he wanted a coat, always,
Asleep or awake.
But this didn't fit so well.

Wearing the new rich tweed coat,
Bought never never,
He was found breathing death in,
Rich rosy skin, at last and forever.
But he couldn't wear that coat in here.
Been inside he had, in his own pad.
Now here I am, cold as well, no-one
To bum a few quid to see me through.
He crossed the line: temptation grew.
Now I stand in that desperate queue.

Shedding

You take it off, that load from life.
It's all bagged and logged, down to the shreds.
Crumpled paper, useless coins, receipts.
Like that one from Bag-a-Bun, some shithole
For a condemned man's last hearty meal.

You're a bag and a sheet of paper, emptied
By questions and commands, and the pretence
That this is a house of care when your
Tired and ragged selfhood is shed away
Like that excess fat now hugging your brain.

Reception

*'They brought in this guy,
cripple he was, handcuffed!
Like he was gonna hop it!'*

Box

He was never meant to be in there,
In nothing but a box. He told them so.
Shouting, he tried that. Then sulking.
Nothing left then but staring, cutting off.
No choice, like sardines. Boxed and slimy.
There had been words of advice from screws.
Words cooing and lecturing, by turns.
No consolation, not except for peace.
He had wanted that, but never said so.

Arms

Patted, consoled, rewarded, showed he was a mate.
Right bruv? No worries. No questions asked.
Being outside, feeling wrong, sure a natural state;
True feelings hidden, real face masked.

But now nothing but the shouts, the cries;
Now no favours, no wanting, no tears.
Now days, endless as the squares of skies,
Silent as the terrors and the fears.

Wing

*'When I first came in here,
it was bedlam...'*

Storybook Dads on B Wing

I fumble with the mini-disc player,
Reach high for the socket
(It's used for hair-cuts)
The flexes are knotted, and behind us,
As we crouch in a corner,
Cells are opened, it's like falling timber.
Officers bellow out exercise time.
Dad chooses a story to read and send home.
He's nervous, choosing between *Aladdin*
And *The Badger's Bath*. Wearing his grey track-suit,
He is not like dad. At visits though, it's his face

That matters. Now it's his voice,
At first quiet, shaky, hesitant.
But now we're into the badger's story
I'm not there anymore; it's him and daughter.
'Hello Rachel, it's your dad here.
I love you, and I want to read you this.
Love, dad.'
He reads, then stops. 'I can't do this!'
But I urge him on and smile.
He almost chews the mike to hide the noise.

For five minutes, I'm not there at all
And he's not doing time. Carefree, he ends with a song.
'I made that one up. She likes songs.'
I carry away eight minutes of happiness.
Never thought you could measure that.

Doing Time

I'll do it so it stays done.
The enemy, a shadow over the need to forget.
A weed you spray every week,
Looking for its root.
But I'll make every hour pay for that,
Stretch the minutes on a rack.
It's them or me in here.

Symphony of sound? No, an atonal mess.
Keys and chains, doors like tombs.
Some engineers are evil bastards.
Like, once this space was open fields.
I think of the bones beneath.

A wing, now a tunnel of echoes.
You feel the darkness like a shroud.
And here they once walked to endless night,
From chapel to the final box,
A step into never, locked up for good.

The Listener's Turn

It's all a matter of keeping shtumm.
Their words pour out like a split bean-bag.
And this is so far down, this place they've come;
First-timers see me as just the right old lag
To nod and smile, lend a book or a mag.
But most of all to be still, seriously dumb.

I used to talk every minute inside:
Nerves and fears jerked me like a rag doll.
In here there's no place to hide
And the midnight shiver takes its toll
As you burrow down into moonlight's sorry hole.
That's why I can listen, see: I always lied.
Never thought I was a Samaritan, though bad:
Sitting and smiling with an edgy poor coper.
Some of me old mates might think me sad,
But they never knew once I'd been a no-hoper,

A body full of fibs, a feckless soft-soaper;
Now I'm giving back time, something I never had.

Face to Face

Listening? Well it's not a confessional. Best eye-to-eye,
and face-to-face makes all the words stay noticed.
So that's my role here, Listener. The ear on the wings,
But truth is, watching the lips move and the eyes betray
is just one thing. Mainly, you're like a cougar
in a jungle, every inch of you tuned to sense customers.

Some sneak in, whispering, after jabbing your arm.
Others write it on the app, in too many words.
The worst cases have faces that show the damage.
They all know I'm one of them, been through it,
Got the tablets to prove it, know the right words.
Best of all, they know I shut it and welcome them.

There is training, yes. I watched films. Role-played,
heard the professionals explain danger signs.
The long words were forgotten; Anglo-Saxon stays.
What are they, these lost souls? They're me and you.
All their distractions come out as lies, comforting;
All their truths stay locked inside, safe as a stash.

I say to them *don't ask me for fancy words, knowing nods.*
Pretend you're talking to yourself, like you do at midnight.
Then see yourself locking all this shit into a box,
Hammering in the nails, and leaving it on a shelf.
Call it the *box of forgetting* because memory is toxic.

Yes, there are tricks, techniques, strategies. My pad
Has a few feet of paper with guiding principles.
But the ones never seen in the rule-book live here:

In my head, shut away and always ready to show off.
The real hurdle is blokes themselves. We feel scared of words.
Except for the few workable, survival words, the ones used to win,
or to survive, and most of all to pretend. We are skilled at fabrications.

Someone sat me down once, in this mad-house, and she listened;
never said a word until I stopped and shuddered as sobs
shook me to a standstill. *I'd like to do what you do, Miss.*
She gave me a smile. I think I made her day. We shook hands.

So I listen: smile, nod, pull faces, express sympathy,
and at the end of my day I feel some of the burden gone.
Maybe some of theirs falls away too. Sometimes they tell me.

My first years inside, I felt the hope fade away like dew.
I remember the feeling: lost in an endless forest, the dark
moving in to choke out the light, the way. I sensed the grip
at my throat. I had to write about that once. Finding truth.

The stretch inside can seem like that forest. No road signs,
No directions and nobody to ask about destinations.
I guess that's what I am in here: a road sign, hoping
my words are right, my reassurance honest as the face they see.

Pad

*'A box with
a window
for giraffes'*

Pad

I have had to make my own skies in here.
Staring towards the wings of struggling pigeons,
I wait for a vision, to see what no-one else sees.
Because this is oblivion, a mind in a void.

Days are like those endless American highways:
Like the driver, my head lilts and falls.

When I was a kid, I was taken to a zoo.
My heart thumping in my throat, I watched the liger
And the tigon, each a hybrid rage in a few square feet.
They walked their stinky few steps, heads shaking,
Eyes strange but dead like gooseberries.

Pad, pad, pad. That's in my head now.
I'm walking and wishing kids could stare at me,
As a wonder, something from their low imaginings.

A Room with no Mirrors

Sometimes, you ask yourself,
What do you fear the most?
Maybe a room with no mirrors,
Then every space you occupy becomes a cell.

Nowhere to see the latest face.
Nowhere to check on what life does.
No-one to verify who you are.

Last thing you do before leaving,
Glance in the mirror. No toothpaste smudge.

But for some the glass has Mr Hyde.
Better not to look.

Three of Us

There are three of us in this place;
Two are well-known and play their part.
The first performs and smiles for all;
The second changes on command.
But the third one no-one sees: a face
Made for this box, not for the public part.
The two outside are walking tall,
Stepping out in unknown land;
The third one knows it's weak and small.

Out There

Out there is the language of love.
Sweet, like a first confession.
I've reached for it, heard its words
Beyond the bars.

I want it to out-talk jailbird words,
They are the dictionary of despair.

All around me are grunts,
The rages, the hatred.
They taught me the dead words.

But all the time in this tip,
I knew that words about love existed.

One time his piss from the bunk above
Dripped on my writing pad.
But that didn't stink them out, the words.
Always sweet, the language of love.

His Eyes

His eyes were a sad blue like my son's.
He sat in a plastic chair,
A new arrival on the wing.
I responded to a note and paid a call,
Feeling like the word doctor.
He told the story, eyes gleaming,
With new tears.
Garbled, anxious, it was a one-way
System signposted remorse.
It was dark... I suppose I was distracted
The officers said it could not be my fault.
So we sit, surrounded by well-meaning
Literature about heroin and sadness.
And I nod, knowing he has told
This fractured narrative endlessly,
On a loop from the sick heart.

He had walked to look, seen
His body starred on the asphalt
Ambered by the street light
His eyes were a sad blue like my son's.

Workshop

'Bloody nets for goals... I ask you!
Some sick joke or what?
I feel like jumping in it,
and get tangled up
like the goalie in a park match...

Stuff

Making stuff with my hands
But make believe in my head.
Making do in foreign lands,
Like these old rooms among the dead.
Stuff, for what?
For them with less than we got.
Maybe I'd swap with that lot,
Out there, with gruel in a flower-pot.

On Domestics

That walk across the asphalt from gate to gate:
It's like when a van spills its load on a motorway.
A great surge of colours, fruit, yoghurt cartons,
Underpants, socks, baked beans, bog roll,
Cartons of chips, screwed-up letters that failed.

This is rats' paradise. I find myself looking
At walls for the wet smears of their runs,
The rats, shyer than any man here. More careful.

And some poor sod has to clean it all up.
The domestic party head out, like trench-diggers
Into no-man's land, shovels and bags ready.
All I think about, treading nimbly over lost hopes,
Trying hard not to stand hard on a dead love,
Is how it tells us what it is to be lost, half mad.

Library

*'To the reader of this book:
Greeny, A Wing, is a grass.'*

*'If this book should chance to roam,
Smack its bum and send it home.'*

In the Library, Saturday

Here they come again, a steady trail of men in grey.
They come from grey boxes, wearing grey cotton.
Faces grey with being inside too long, too deep.
Is there anything here to assuage the seeping boredom?

One fingers a solid fantasy novel. Another stares, gawping
At a wall of red. This is called True Crime.
He weaves dreams of gangster capers, jail tales.

No talking as a rule but I'm there to stir some up.
The young man decides on something about Hard Men.
This wakes up an officer, a man disciplined to stillness.
But he says, 'Hard... hey son, I'll tell you hard.
We had a hit-man here once. Used to pull out his finger-nails
in front of you. For a response, like. That's hard.'

'No shit?' asks the kid. His book is stamped, but all eyes
are on the officer, who allows a broad smile.
'Never gave him a response though. He hated that.'

The Boston Boy

The poetry books are smeared and smudged,
Ruined by blokes whose hearts haven't budged.

The Boston Boy was brave with drink;
He just lashed out: he didn't think.
Eliot understood the pressure to act,
To flap like seaweed under water
As each new flood engulfs you.

But here a poet sells his poses;
Has to talk of vows, promises,
Sorrowful regrets and red, red roses.

The Boston Boy came home one day
To find his girl had gone away

Here the words reach like hands for alms,
Beggars in some skid row lined
With failed men who trod the wrong board
But somehow the poems still live,
Go into the world like Mayday notes

The Boston Boy sat alone in his cell,
Blaming no-one for making his Hell.

The Quiet Guy

Down on ones they're playing bowls, kids' playgroup style.
Even throwing darts – soft-headed – onto a sticky board.
Some of the cons, reason gone, still laugh and smile;
One or two find a prayer for their Lord.
Me, I'm the quiet guy who kills the time.
I'm the one who doesn't do friendship. I made that clear.
Spelled it out to every bloke, first day in here.

In a side-room the scrots all yell at a screen.
Their nick-names come from films like *Shrek*;
They can't move from the fun of seventeen.
They still love the guy who's got some neck.
I'm the quiet guy who kills the time.
I'm the one keeps his head down, his trust near;
Laid down the law along the wing, dished out with fear.

Down on the ones they're watching me, checking me out.
Some wink when they see me watch their play;
Just one cocky lad tries a gesture, throws a shout
into the stench of another stale day.
I'm the quiet guy who kills the time
Yes, I'm the one whose name comes dear;
I laid down that law, first day in here.

If you don't need the other guy, so I was told,
You'll stay strong, rely on number one.
Warm yourself, let the other guy go cold
The other man's problems weigh a ton.
I'm the quiet guy who kills the time.
Me, I'm the one runs light and free, in my head,
but if I stopped breathing, would they know I was dead?

Gym

'I lose myself in here...
glad to do it bruv.'

Place

This great solid box, standing there
Like something dropped from that wide sky
Making Lincolnshire and endless dream;
Magic box? Memory box?
Maybe a room, a House of Pain?
All, all wrong-headed. No, this is a retreat.
Truth is, all this flexing and straining,
It's closer to a monkish cell than confinement.
I think of the Book of Days, a calendar
And here the days are ticked off,
Dressed down, just for being too much there.

Weights

He ain't heavy – he's my brother

Wealth, as the Romans had it, was *impedimenta*
Things are nice, but change from smiles to burdens.
Here, off Greetwell Road, what you have is small,
Enough to feed routine and placate the boredom.
People need to carry burdens, in the end:
To prove something to themselves about being here,
Where just waking up presents a puzzle every day,
And finding the right pieces at the right time
Leaves us with our childish tempers or invites
That guy Mr Hyde who lives in our minds' cellars,
To pay a call and take the weight off our minds.

Better to have a burden you can boss, like a wheel.
And they squat there in the room by the gym:
Like huge discarded wheels from some failed engine.
Go on, fifteen K... bit more. I'm behind you. I'm here.
There's a burden we yearn for, weep for: a friend.

The Lads

Funny how you find some rest inside when
You squat and lift, your face close to the wall mirror,
And all you ask of that complicated bloke there
Is that he thinks of nothing but this moment.

Funny how men need so little from each other.
Few words required, maybe a nod and a nudge.
All they ask is some smiles and ribbing
To reassure them that they belong somewhere.

Funny how the landscape changes when there's only you,
Just this body, to take care of; the weather stays the same.
The weekdays all fall in line and become Sameday.
Days won't do as they're told, but then you don't care.

Funny how lads together long for the changing room jokes.
As long as some other lad has the laugh on him, fine.
But here, the star turns are the storytelling blokes:
The lads who crease your face when you stand in line.

Escape

Now there's a word to bring a shiver to the spine.
The bog-cleaner in Samarkand wants to escape to Wigan.
Maybe the souls in Heaven long for a day in Hell.
They've heard that Adolf Hitler's there, arm-wrestling
With Vlad the Impaler while Joe Stalin drinks vodka.

But the best escape is into the geography inside,
Not the mad race to the seaside or the caravan.
Like here, as you sweat and pull, lift and strain,
The road you take is the highway through pain.

You work through numbers in your head,
Going to where you can beat your best to date;
Yes, the best escape, as a great poet once said,
Is to a place where you really enjoyed the wait.

Block

'Ever wondered what a monk
did to fill his time, pal?'

One Wrong Move

They used to say it in the B movies,
Like when Cagney or Bogie pulled a gun.
A grimace on the face, a sneer of command.

One wrong move and you're history.
Move a finger or a lip and you know what?
You'll have a belly full of lead.

But no laughs now when I sit here wringing
My hands, struggling to find words that match
The brain-ache inside, where that place hurts,
The little pocket in the mind that decides,
Most times the right choice. Like buy or sell,
Green or red? Jeans or trousers? Love or fear?

But then, after a million little choices,
Right for the time, there comes a bad one.
Some words found their way to my lips, a lapse
Of normal thought, a drop too much wine

At the wrong hour with the wrong person.
Moments clicked together to forge the chain.
No going back. Like when you leave the house
And leave the wallet, sensing a panic as you board the plane.

One wrong move and you're history.
My dreams in this magnolia cream box
Are of Bogie's face, Cagney's pained face.
Son, at twenty three, that was a bad move.

Have to do what has to be done,
Son. So I'm searching for the spot
Where the wrong words lived. To flush them out.
Before I screw up another life.

Nutjob

Oh the ache in my head, the raven's beak,
Is here again, where I cannot speak.
Talk to yourself and sort things out,
So one guy said, a stranger to doubt.
The screws see me as one prime nutjob,
Here among many, alone, who sob
And whine for what they were, not are:
Here where peace is much too far
To reach for and hold, from this deep dark;
A beautiful thought, like a rising lark.

Beyond the Bars

The battlefield has shrunk to this:
My pad in the local jail.
The fight was once in khaki, next door to hell;
Now it's here in this sweat-box cell.

But I always looked beyond the bars,
Out of the darkness and up to the stars.
I know my buddies spin out of time
Those gone before, who gave their lives,
And left at home their kids and wives.
I talk to them and share their song,
The ones who died to right a wrong.

My army kit has shrunk to this:
Sweatshirt, jeans and prison wear.
The fight was once a kid's fine dream
Of being one who makes the team.

The days are long and the nights are longer
But love beats hate and makes me stronger.
The terrors of peace messed with my head,
But one day I'll beat this fear and dread,
And nothing done in the cause of right
Can shift these words, still shining bright:

I always looked beyond the bars
Out of the darkness and up to the stars.

Never Had a Dream

Here, the stink of who came before.
Spat, shit, could say that, thinking of brutes.
They surely dreamed of beyond the door:
Women, bread, pissed as newts.
Being helpless, legless, feckless,
Abandoned and stupidly reckless.

Me? If I had a dream, it never stuck.
Never scored the winner.
Never swung the fists, into the ruck.
Never saw the sun. Guess I'm a sinner.

But still, I was left alone, to think.
I imagined the block papered, pink with flowers;
I saw the walls melt, with my imaginary powers.

Last One

In this pad
Good time I had
Seven years tops
I'm lovin' it
Top of the pops
Mate.

The Ballad of Hull Prison

Some say I never think, some say I never try.
My lover says I lost her, threw our life away;
All I know for sure is that the past has been a lie.
I've traded hot ambition for a square of Hedon sky.

Some say I'm not to blame, that love has said goodbye;
Some say I didn't do wrong, I just lost my way.
Now I know what it's like to sit and sigh:
I've traded hot ambition for a square of Hedon sky

Didn't need no gun, didn't need no knife, I was high.
Cut my life down dead, and there's no words to say.
A thousand people ask me when and who and why
I've traded hot ambition for a square of Hedon sky.

The Poet's Farewell, or Dylan Thomas Drank Here

That sheet of paper, in the boat-house:
Four words and a blot. Three more words
And a beer-stain.
That's work, that is. A poet's work.

He sat here and he sat there;
He kissed so many lips goodbye.
When he kissed his last Muse farewell,
Did he regret the blots, the drips, the stains?

No, Dylan Thomas drank here. Preferred beer.
Would take wine and whisky if pushed.
So what we have is notebooks, rough drafts,
Words sailing without forrards or without afts.

But whatever vessels set him free, he loved their
Fragments, as he wanted a share in their journeys.

That sheet of paper, on the bar-room table, that's work,
That is, with the blot, the stain, or no, no: it's sweat.
He never believed that the last was the best he would get.

And I wrote in here, hunched at a desk,
In the prison library, was I making sense of nonsense,
Or nonsense out of sense? I'm with you, Dylan,
Let the bottle decide, with its answers hidden
Like the desperate jail hooch, squat in the chapel.

Out

*'I've got certificates from inside
basic this and that
but nothing that says I changed.
You'll have to believe an old lag...'*

No Walls

I'm used to walls. They keep you out and me in.
I left all my thoughts inside, enough to last the eternal ride.
I'm used to walls. They stay where they are;
They keep still but my nut goes far.
Now I'm out, the world's come back, and that's too hard.
It went away, never sent me a card.
I'm used to walls. They never tell you you're no good.
Outside it's never *can* and *will*: it's always *should*.

Winding Lane Blues

Thinking of Robert Southwell

The sorest wight may find relief of pain
And we're all caught on that winding lane.
I'm praying this time will never come again,
Oh Lord, I'm on that winding lane.

Can't see ahead, just a dark corner turns away;
Can't see nothing, and lost for what to say.
We're all working hard to stay safe and sane.
Oh Lord, I'm on that winding lane.

Looking back hurts, and losing folk is hard;
The fight goes on, keep up that guard.
I'm praying this time will never come again,
Oh Lord, I'm on that winding lane.

I screw up my eyes to see the road ahead;
I know I can't sleep, but still go to my bed.
We're all caught on that winding lane,
And it's better to sing than sit and complain.

So we're all caught on that winding lane;
The dark troubles every soul on that road,
But I'm praying this time will never come again.
Oh Lord, I'm on that winding lane.

But I'm grateful for my loved ones' smiles
As life goes on, tough miles on miles;
The sorest wight may find relief of pain,
And I'm looking to the end of that winding lane.

Out

Now he was out again. Where he felt the air, the burn.
He was always out: the building, the room, the class.
of step, for the count, caught lbw by life's wicket-keeper.
Of dosh, of bread, speaking out of turn even;
of options, choices; of ideas, alternatives, in the cold.
When he was *in*, it was for the smallest cut,
In on the plan, in with the crowd, in favour.
But then it came to *in the way*...

So he was out again. He liked that. Being out
Meant he was not to be found, not traced,
In the shadows, like. Comfortable, being out.
See, when the bills dropped and when the pigs called,
He was out. The best out of the lot: out of the picture.

Left Behind

When I came in this place I dragged a prison issue
large plastic bag; there was the lot in there- proof.
I mean proof that I done something. I'd tried to be new.
Tried to be different, sing and not moan under that roof.
Now I'm walking out, what's left behind of me?
I'm just one more con what's moved on, forgotten.
I guess I tried to make them listen, make them see
That I went inside bad but not lost, not rotten.
No, nothing left in there of yours truly, no smell,
No sounds, no echoes, no wisdom and no speeches;
But no man can say in that shithole I raised hell.
No, *that* I took in with me, and brought it out as well.

The Shade

I saw it once, down a dark landing, and again
Just a shadow waiting to talk, but frustrated.
It was the shade in my underworld, for ever
Failing to be seen and heard, something never
In my life but treading around it, lost and hated.
I felt it once, a fleeting, nagging pain
Pulling at my chest, telling me yet again
That it had been behind, and waited, waited.

I sensed it once, a passing shadow over my bed.
Just a second of comfort, no more than a whisper.
Still the shade of my underworld, wanting a smile.
But I knew its tricks, its cons, its guile.
Never a bold word, louder, sharper, crisper.

No, I never spoke a word to such a ghost,
Trying to tell me what I wanted most:
Some strand of truth in life to weave in,
Some remnant of me to keep, to believe in.

My One Good Suit

What I left in there:
Two paperbacks stained with cheap tea;
A plastic mug, chipped,
A drawing by Taff, *A Choppy Sea*,
And one of me: tired and tight-lipped.

A feast of memory, now only crumbs;
Countless hours of sulks and moods
Spent with wasters, rogues and bums.
Days of listening to dead-end dudes.

But worst of all I left my youth,
With all the seductive dreams,
Rubbed out by unwelcome truth.
My one good suit, gone at the seams.